JOYFUL REUNION

by
Jim Ertel

And God shall wipe away all tears from their eyes; and there will be no more death, or sorrow, or crying, or pain; for the former things have passed away.

Revelation 21:4

(author paraphrase)

Joyful Reunion
ISBN: 978-1-60683-650-7

Copyright ©2012 James Ertel
P.O. Box 2063
Monument, CO 80132

Published by Harrison House, Inc.
P.O. Box 35035
Tulsa, OK 74153
www.HarrisonHouse.com

JOYFUL REUNION

Tick, tock. Tick, tock. The hypnotic ticking of the grand-father clock kept perfect beat with the rhythm of Kim's heart. The quietness was nearly deafening to her as she sat motionless in the corner of the sofa. Wrapped in a cozy fleece blanket with her legs tucked under her, she had long forgotten about the caramel latte she had barely touched. Instead, she stared mindlessly out the bay window. The sun had just settled below the horizon, silhouetting the majes-tic snow-covered peaks against a deep-blue cloudless sky. But it wasn't the calm beauty of the evening that held her captive; it was the fear that a storm might be coming— one of her own making.

Tonight, Kim would reveal a secret to Mike she had kept hidden for nearly a decade. She had desperately tried to keep the memory of this secret locked away in a dark closet, deep in the recesses of her mind and as far from the wounds of her heart as possible. But in the late night hours her dreams would often defy her will, releasing the pain and heartache again and again.

Until yesterday, her lifelong friend, Amy, was the only other person who knew the truth, and Amy was willing to take that knowledge with her to the grave. There was good reason for keeping this secret and no good reason to reveal it. Until now. A life-changing revelation had emerged through the fog of brokenness and fear that finally gave Kim the reason, the courage really, to expose her secret to the light. Would Mike understand? Would he ever trust her again? She hoped so. She prayed so.

In the midst of the fears and doubts, Kim's mind was flooded with memories. She thought about her first conversation with Mike. She couldn't pinpoint the week or month, but it was definitely on a Friday afternoon sometime in the fall of 2002. That was her senior year in high school, and she remembered being dressed in her blue and gold "Go Wildcats" uniform that the cheerleaders always wore on Fridays for the student body football rally. The memory of the first time she met Mike shot into her mind: She was tossing her books in the locker before heading to the Friday pep rally when Mike nervously approached. She had hardly noticed the lanky, insecure late bloomer until this moment when she realized with horror that he was about to ask her out.

"Would you like to go out for pizza after the game?" he asked timidly.

Kim pretended not to hear him while at the same time looking around, hoping that no one else had heard him either. When he stepped closer and repeated the question, she took a deep breath and sighed, and then completely destroyed any flicker of hope he may have had with four sarcastic words: "Are you kidding me?"

Turning, she tossed her long blonde hair to one side and walked away. It worked. He never asked again.

Kim had big plans, and they certainly didn't include someone like Mike. The following spring she was accepted to an Ivy League school known for their excellent teachers' program. From the time she was a young girl she had dreamed of becoming a teacher, and now she would have the opportunity to pursue that dream. She couldn't wait to say goodbye to the boring little town she had grown up in, population 13,500. She was sure God had reserved Elk Grove for hicks and losers. How could she possibly live in a place where a romantic evening consisted of three slices of pepperoni pizza at Poppa's Pizza followed by two fun-filled hours at Billy's Bowling World?

Even more appealing than attending college was knowing that for nine months of each of the next four years, she would be four hundred miles away from her father's relentless demands for perfection. He took great pride in having served as a city councilman for many years, and as he put it, "We have a public image to protect within the community." He was sure that everyone in town was watching him, and the last thing he needed was to be embarrassed by his daughter's behavior.

He never failed to remind Kim how important this was. "Elk Grove is a small town," he would say. "There are no secrets here." And it was true; when the gossip mill was in full swing, every titillating detail of a person's private life eventually became public knowledge, or so it seemed. Perhaps that explained his reason for encouraging Kim to attend church with her mother.

Christmas and Easter were the only two days of the year that he would even consider darkening the doors of a church himself. Kim could never quite figure it out. Did he go to please her mother, or was it to be seen by members of the community? She leaned toward the latter. Whatever his motive for going, her mother's was genuine. She loved God, she loved her friends in the church, and she drew strength from worshiping there. Kim couldn't remember a single Sunday that didn't include Sunday school when she was growing up because her mom would have it no other way.

All her life Kim had tried her best to please her father. She could still remember sitting at the kitchen table as a little girl, working diligently on an artistic masterpiece of shapes and colors for Daddy. When it was finished, she printed her name with the brightest blue crayon she could find, and then dashed into the living room where she bounded into his lap. "Look, Daddy. Look how I stayed inside the lines."

"That's nice," he said, with a cursory glance, and then sent her away to play. Her mother, sensing Kim's disappointment, took the drawing into the kitchen and hung it in the center of the refrigerator door with a magnet. "It's beautiful, honey. Daddy will be able to see it every day if we put it here."

As Kim grew older, she focused on her studies with the goal of getting the best grades in the class. In junior and senior high, her reading light was seldom out before eleven. She hoped that if she studied hard enough, she could earn his approval. The result of her diligence was exceptional grades that would serve her well in the future. As for her father, he never gave her more than a smile and a peck on the cheek for a good report card.

By the time Kim graduated from high school she had concluded that her father's expectations were, for the most part, simply unattainable. Were it not for the love of her mother, his constant reminders of her inadequacies would have driven Kim away much sooner. Yet, he was still her father, and she clung to the hope that one day she would meet with his approval and finally receive the love and affection that she craved from him.

There were only two people who Kim knew she would really miss while away at college. One was her mother and the other was her best friend, Amy. She and Amy were kindred spirits and nearly inseparable since grade school. When they were twelve, they created for themselves a secret hiding place in the attic of Amy's house. Late one night during a sleepover, they quietly made their way up the narrow stairs to the attic, where by the light of a single candle they made a solemn pledge to each other, one that only true friends could make: "Always the truth, never a secret." To this day that pledge has never been broken.

In their sophomore year of high school they made another pledge, one that many of their girlfriends could no longer make, and one they knew might not stand the test of time. But with as much resolve and determination as they could muster, they made the pledge anyway: "We promise to keep ourselves for our one true love, the man we will marry."

Although their lives would be going in different directions after high school, this was a friendship they knew would endure. What neither of them could have possibly known was that it would soon become the only lifeline holding Kim's head above water in a stormy sea.

A few days before Kim left for college, she and her mother decided the two of them had better sort through everything in Kim's room. They emptied the contents of the dresser drawers on the floor, took all the clothes out of the closet and laid them across the bed and even brought the storage boxes from the basement to her room. Piles of clothes, a mountain of shoes, and more were strewn everywhere as they tried to decide what should stay and what should go. They looked at each other for a moment and then burst into laughter.

"Look what we've done," Kim said.

"I know. It's a mess, isn't it?" her mother replied.

Exhausted, they dropped to the floor where they were forced to sit crossed legged in the only available space, a small spot next to the luggage, and just big enough for the two of them.

"Oh well, at least we're making a memory. Right, Mom?" It was an old cliché, but one that Kim and her mom liked to use when one of them felt they were in the midst of a special time together. Her mother didn't respond with words, she just looked at Kim and smiled in a way that communicated deep love and heartache at the same time. Tears welled up in her eyes as she put her arms around Kim. Hugging her neck tightly with her cheek pressed against Kim's, she gently stroked the back of Kim's head. It was an expression of reassuring love that had comforted Kim many times before. "Kim," her mother whispered, "I know it hasn't always been easy for you here, and I'm so sorry for that. I will miss you more than you can possibly know, but now, this is your opportunity to start your own life, and I'm excited for you."

They slowly released their hug, and then Kim took one of her mother's hands and held it gently in both of hers. "Will you be okay without me, Mom?"

"Yes, I will." Her mother paused, then continued, "I know what you're thinking, and I love you for it. But you don't need to worry. Deep down, your father is a good man, and whether you understand it or not, I want you to know that I love him. Without him, I wouldn't have had the joy of loving you these last nineteen years. And even though your father seldom shows it, I know he loves you."

"Well maybe so, but whether he does or not, I have never doubted your love, Mom. I'll miss you."

———————◦◦◦◦———————

Kim and her mother had made the four hundred-mile trek to the college town together twice before. Once, years earlier for a shopping spree, and more recently for a scouting trip to help Kim get the lay of the land. But to-day, there wasn't enough space left in Kim's Honda Civic for a pair of tennis shoes, much less another passenger. And besides, this time it was a trip that Kim wanted to make alone.

Kim gave her mother one last hug, and then turned to her father, who, to her surprise, actually looked sad. There weren't any tears with his goodbye, of course; just a warm smile followed by a mini-hug and an "I'll miss you" that actually sounded genuine. *Perhaps Mom was right; maybe he does love me,* she thought for one fleeting moment.

Then, as Kim was pulling away, he just had to say it: "Remember, don't do anything your mother and I will be ashamed of." To a casual observer, those words would have sounded like nothing more than a lighthearted parting re-mark. To Kim, they carried with them a heavy burden of expected behaviors and rules, which if broken, never failed to bring down the gavel of judgment and condemnation. So much so, that in the years to come they worked like a giant padlock that would keep the door to her painful secret closed.

One cheeseburger with fries, two soft drinks, a bag of peanuts, and three potty breaks later, Kim pulled over and parked in front of a three-story complex. She was not at all fond of the dorm-room scenario and much preferred the idea of living alone. So, months earlier she went online and found this furnished studio apartment three blocks from the college.

It felt so good to stand up and stretch as she stepped out of the car. The memory foam in the driver's seat had long since lost its memory, and the trip felt like it would never end. "This looks like the place," she said to herself . "I sure hope it's as good as the pictures."

She found the key under the doormat, right where the landlord said it would be. With nervous anticipation, she opened the door to her first apartment. *What is that awful smell?* she thought, taking her first steps inside. Later that night in a call to Amy, she would say it smelled like a mouse had died happily in a lump of moldy limburger cheese. She walked slowly through her two-room studio trying to locate the source of the odor. What she discovered was far less dramatic than she had imagined. A trash bag, nearly full of what slightly resembled rotten vegetables, had been left open under the kitchen sink. Mystery solved, she took out the stinky trash and opened the only two windows to air out the rooms. Aside from the very limited space, if felt good to have her own place.

Kim began to unload the car. The fourteen steps from the first to the second floor were only a nuisance at first, but by trip number twelve they had become a source of pain that would eventually turn her legs to jelly. She pressed on, however, and by ten o'clock the smell was gone, the car was unloaded and she had accomplished the most important chore of all—a thorough scrubbing of the bathtub.

Kim poured an ice-cold Pepsi into the only glass she had taken the time to wash, grabbed her cell phone and a candle, and headed for the bathroom—all of four steps away. Before the tub was full, the fragrance from the candle had permeated the entire apartment. She held onto the towel rack for balance while testing the water temperature with a big toe. Satisfied that it was just right, she stepped in, sat for a moment, and then with a sigh of relief slowly leaned back, sliding further under the water until the bubbles tickled her chin. It was time for a long conversation with Amy that would end the day; everything else could wait until morning.

The first few weeks of college were a blur. Registration was far more complicated than she had imagined. Course selection was a nightmare, even though she had already determined that her major would be education. Hunting down used text books had her running from one end of the campus to the other, then, of all things, she actually had to attend class.

The amount of work her professors assigned was overwhelming. Kim was thankful that she wouldn't be reading the Help Wanted ads this year. She had earned a partial scholarship with her 4.0 grade point average, and her father had promised he would cover the rest of her expenses. Fortunately, he was a believer in the importance of a good education and said he felt a responsibility to help her. He was big on people keeping their word and fulfilling their obligations, with the emphasis on obligations.

Kim's busy schedule left little time for much of anything, but she always found time for long talks with Amy.

"Hi Amy, it's me."

"Hi Kim, how's your week going?"

"Well, I finally figured out the shortest distance between classes; that's a plus."

"Yeah, well, we both know you're directionally challenged. Have you had a chance to get to know anyone yet?"

"Ha, ha, ha, I know how your devious little mind works, Amy. You want to know if I've met any cute guys yet, right?"

"Well, have you?"

It was the second day of her American Lit class. He was sitting one row behind and six or seven chairs to

Kim's right, just within her peripheral vision, allowing her to see him without an obvious turn of the head. She couldn't help but notice that he was staring at her during most of the class. It was a little unnerving, yet flattering at the same time. When class ended, Kim gathered her belongings, all the while acting as though she didn't notice him making his way toward her.

"I don't think we've met. I'm Nathan Whitaker," he said confidently.

"Oh, hi, I'm Kim Erickson."

"Well, it's nice to meet you Kim Erickson. Do you have another class right away? If you don't, I was wondering if you would like to join me for coffee at the Starbucks across the street."

"Well, I guess that would be okay. I could use a caffeine pick-me-up right now. Sure," she replied.

Nathan was president and a founding member of the exclusive, men-only, D.E.O. club. He and five of his buddies had formed the club in their freshman year, complete with bylaws and a formal application process. Three of the Sexy Six, as they liked to call themselves, which included Nathan, had attended prep school together in Cape Cod, Massachusetts, and it was there that the original idea for the club was hatched. Membership was limited, and all applicants were sworn to secrecy before they could apply. If they qualified, then a vote was taken. Unanimous approval by all current members was required for acceptance.

The club collected no dues, but only the rich need apply. Nathan's parents had given him a steel-blue 135i BMW convertible for his high school graduation present. The other five of the Sexy Six drove a variety of expensive sports cars as well. No upstanding D.E.O. member would be caught dead driving something as common as a Dodge or Chevy. Unless, of course, it was Viper or Corvette. The last and most important requirement was that they weren't allowed to hold a job. Their social schedule simply wouldn't permit it.

Prep school had served Nathan well, preparing him for college both academically and socially. However, most of the social graces concerning the opposite sex, for better or worse, were passed on to him by upper classmen. Those refinements, combined with his charming personality, Hollywood smile, and boyish good looks could melt the heart of almost any girl—and he knew it.

Kim was a strikingly beautiful woman for sure. In heels, her 5'9" slender frame allowed her to look most men in the eyes without raising her chin. Her blue eyes were accented by long eyelashes and a perfect complexion with little need of makeup. Her soft features, which included a dimple just below each cheek, were framed by long, naturally blonde hair. But then, Nathan never considered dating anyone who didn't first fit that profile. It wasn't her obvious beauty; it was the sweet innocence about her that he found so compelling.

Most of the girls that he knew were falling all over themselves to gain his attention, offering themselves up like groupies at a rock concert. Kim, however, hadn't seemed at all impressed with him at Starbucks. For Nathan, that cool response was like waving a red cape in front of a bull. He realized very quickly that a full-court press would not work with this one, and he would have to resort to the D.E.O. method—Disarm, Empathize, Overcome. It required patience, not one of his strong character traits, but he could afford to wait in this target-rich environment where there was never a lack for companionship.

Starbucks became a regular meeting place for Kim and Nathan that fall. Kim never tired of a hot latte or an iced coffee, and keeping her friendship with Nathan in a public setting felt very comfortable. "My education is too important to be compromised by a serious relationship," she would tell Amy.

"Who are you trying to convince?" was always Amy's reply.

Unlike most boys Kim had known, Nathan seldom talked about himself. He didn't seem at all self-absorbed and much preferred learning about her. "What a refreshing attitude," Kim told Amy in one late night conversation. Latte by latte, Nathan was becoming what she believed to be a true friend and confidant. She was beginning to trust this boy who asked for nothing in return.

If only, she now thought, as tears slowly trickled down her cheeks and dripped unnoticed onto her blanket where they quickly disappeared. *If only I had known then what I know now, I would have ended it right there. How could I have been so blind?* How different these last ten years might have been. So vivid were her memories now that the world around her seemed to fade away; she felt like she was being transported back in time.

Kim was the first to raise the stakes. "Nathan, a friend gave me two tickets to the Main Street Dinner Theater for next Friday night. *Singing in the Rain* is playing. I've always wanted to see it, but I don't want to go alone. Would you come with me?"

"Sure, I'd love to," Nathan replied. "What time shall I pick you up?" Nathan planned his arrival at her apartment fifteen minutes ahead of their agreed time.

"Am I early?" he asked when Kim opened the door.

"Maybe a little; I do need a few more minutes. You can wait inside if you like."

"Thank you, but I'll just wait here by the door if that's okay." They had known each other for several weeks now, so his answer surprised her, although she did think it was kind of sweet.

"Sure, I'll be right out."

They walked to the car where he opened the door and helped her in. It was the beginning of what she would later say was the perfect evening. She was being treated like a princess—a first for her—and she loved it. When they arrived back at her apartment, Nathan maintained the role of gentleman. He unlocked the apartment door and handed her the key.

"I had a great time," Kim said. "Thanks for keeping me company."

"I had a good time, too, Kim. Maybe we could do something like this again. Would that be all right with you?"

"Yeah, I would really like that."

He reached for one of her hands and held it in his. Then he looked in her eyes, waiting for just the right moment. "It really means a lot to me to have a friend like you, Kim. Thank you."

"You're welcome, Nathan. I feel the same way about you."

"I was hoping you did," he said fondly. "But now, it's time for me to go. I'll call you tomorrow." Nathan let her hand slowly slip from his as he turned to walk away.

"Good night," she replied. She closed the door, hung up her coat, and then sat down for a moment to ponder what just happened. He left without the slightest hint that he expected anything more than a simple good-night. How surprising.

"Perhaps Nathan is a kindred spirit," she told Amy. "I feel like I can talk to him about anything."

Indeed, Nathan always listened carefully and thought-fully as she talked about her family, how much she loved her mother, and how unhappy the relationship with her father made her feel. He never seemed to lose interest, not even when she recounted lengthy conversations with Amy. In time, there was very little he didn't know about her. Kim, on the other hand, remained in the dark about many of the details of his life, but it no longer mattered to her. He had won her trust and was now beginning to win her heart.

Nathan could read Kim like a book. When she felt insignificant or unappreciated, he filled her mind and touched her heart with words of praise and approval. When she felt isolated or lonely, he would comfort her with the tender loving affection that she had never received from her father. Their first kiss, which had long since come and gone, was even more romantic than Kim had imagined it would be. Nathan made sure of that. All was working according to plan, and Kim was completely unaware that she was being played like a virtuoso plays a Stradivarius.

Nathan no longer waited outside the door when he picked her up, and he always stayed late after a date. It was one of those late nights when Nathan sensed the time had come; he would play the wild card that would win the game. After one of their many passionate embraces, he got up from the couch and walked to the other side of the room where his coat was hanging. He reached inside a pocket and pulled out a small, royal blue velvet-covered box with gold trim.

Kim's heart began to race as he walked slowly toward her, gazing at her through those puppy dog eyes all the way. He knelt down, and without saying a word, held the box in front of her and slowly opened the lid. Inside was a beautiful set of diamond earrings. She gasped. "Oh, Nathan, they're beautiful!" She stared at them for a few seconds admiring their beauty and then looked up at Nathan.

"Thank you, Nathan, but..." Before she could finish, he put his fingers over her lips.

"Shh. Before you say another word, I must tell you, I've fallen in love with you, Kim."

Late the next morning, Kim picked up the phone and dialed. "Hi Amy, it's Kim. 'Always the truth, never a secret.' Right, Amy?" she said. Those words never failed to peg the needle on the curiosity meter.

"Oh my gosh, Kim. What happened?" she demanded.

"Please don't be upset with me when I tell you this, but I've broken our pledge. Nathan and I made love last night."

There was silence for only a few seconds before Amy replied, but it seemed like an eternity to Kim. "Really? Wow…I'm, I'm…I hardly know what to say, except, well, I guess I'm, like, not totally surprised. You've certainly been spending a lot of time with him in your apartment; I guess it was bound to happen sooner or later."

"Don't be sad for me, and don't worry. He loves me, Amy. He really loves me, and I love him. I'm sure it won't be long before he asks me to marry him."

"Are you sure? Are you really sure you're doing the right thing, Kim?"

"Yes I'm sure. With all my heart."

Kim grabbed the edge of the bathroom sink to steady herself. Heart pounding and feeling lightheaded, Kim felt her knees buckling beneath her. Unable to support her own weight any longer, she slowly lowered herself to the cold tile floor where she collapsed into a fetal position. "Oh my God, it can't be true. Please God, don't let this be true," she cried. But there was no denying it: two strips; and both indicated positive.

Amy always used to tell Kim, "Don't worry; time is your friend. All of this will seem like nothing more than a bad dream one day." How she had hoped Amy was right. But these many years later, the memories of that dreadful night had not dimmed. Sitting on a comfortable sofa wrapped in a warm blanket made little difference. In her mind, she was back on that bathroom floor agonizing over the realization that she was pregnant.

She could remember every detail—the sound of the water draining through the pipes as she lay on the floor, the smell of the cleaners under the sink only inches from her face, and the cold feeling of the tile next to her bare skin. Even more vivid than the sounds and smells was the memory of those haunting words that coursed through her mind over and over and over as she lay on the floor: "Don't do anything your mother and I will be ashamed of."

"Thank God," she whispered, "it is all coming to an end tonight; no longer will those words hold me hostage, no longer will I be afraid, no longer will I be ashamed. No more secrets."

Kim got up from the bathroom floor and slowly made her way across the room to her unmade bed and crawled in. She pulled the covers over her head as though she could hide from the realities of the altered life she would now face. In the dark, the tears slowly subsided as her imagination began to manufacture the solution. *I'll tell Nathan tomorrow,* she thought. *We'll have to marry soon; I won't be able to hide this for long. We can live here for a while but will need a bigger place when the baby comes. I should be able to finish out my freshman year before the baby arrives.* On and on it went until she finally fell asleep.

The next morning, Kim didn't wake until nearly ten o'clock. Nathan was in class by then so she would have to leave a message on his phone. "Nathan, I have to talk to you immediately. Call me as soon as you're out of class."

Eleven o'clock. *He should be out of class by now,* she reasoned. Why hasn't he called?

Twelve o'clock, one o'clock—minutes seemed like hours, and nothing; she called again and repeated the message. Near five, her phone finally rang.

"Nathan, why haven't you returned my calls? I have to talk to you right away!"

"I was busy. What's so important?"

"I can't tell you over the phone. I need to see you."

"Okay, give me about thirty minutes and I'll be there. Bye."

To Nathan, this call sounded like so many others he'd received from girls who felt he owed them something. He hadn't the slightest intention of taking this relationship any further.

Kim was standing near the curb when he pulled up. She opened the door and slid down into the bucket seat.

"So what's the big deal?" he asked impatiently.

She reached for the strip in her coat pocket, took it out, and held it in front of him, not saying a word. Her announcement did not provoke the response from him that she expected. She watched as the blood rushed from his face, leaving his skin pale. It took a moment for the boy who had seemed so confident and unflappable to regain his composure and respond.

"I told you condoms don't always work. Why didn't you get on the pill like I asked?"

"I don't know. I just didn't. But I am pregnant, there's no doubt. We're going to have a baby, Nathan."

"No we're not," he said, as though he held the power to control her every decision. "I can promise you that, Kim."

The charming boy she had come to know suddenly changed. It was as though some evil being filled with hate was looking at her through his eyes. She felt chilled as shivers coursed up her spine.

"What are you saying?" she asked.

"I'm saying you're going to get an abortion! I'm not about to be a father, and you are certainly not ready to be a mother. If you think I'm going to ruin my life by bringing some whinny kid into this world, then think again."

"Nathan! How can you ask me to do that? It's wrong. There has got to be another solution."

"No! There's not." His words seemed almost threatening. "What are you thinking? Are you expecting me to marry you now? You're so naïve Kim. You just don't get it, do you? That is never going to happen."

Sobbing, Kim reached for his hand and gripped it tightly, desperate for the compassion and comfort he had so willingly offered before. There was none to be found. He jerked his hand away.

"Nathan, you told me you loved me. Was that all a lie?"

"Look Kim, I don't even know for sure if it's my baby."

Kim's heart was breaking, she could take no more. She forced herself to open the door and step to the curb. Then she turned around—looking, hoping, and longing for something, anything to ease the unbearable pain inside. Instead, Nathan served up one final blow.

He grinned at Kim in a sadistically gleeful way that frightened her. "Look Kim," he said, "just calm down. It's not all that bad; no one but the two of us will ever know. And you don't need to worry about the money. I'll pay for the abortion. It wouldn't be the first time and maybe not the last." With that, he threw the strip out of the car, slammed the door, and sped away. Kim was left standing on the curb, tossed aside like the pregnancy test strip lying in the gutter.

The short walk to her apartment seemed like an eternity. It took every ounce of her strength that remained. By the time Kim reached her door, she began convulsing, throwing up on herself, the carpet, and the mat by the door. But it didn't matter; she felt like dying.

When the vomiting subsided, she slowly regained enough strength to get up on all fours and crawl to the bathroom where she began stripping off her clothes. "Amy...I've got to talk to Amy." She crawled back into the living room where she fumbled through her purse looking for the cell phone. She pressed the number one on speed dial, and the phone began to ring. "Pick up Amy, pick up," she pleaded.

"Hi Kim, what's up?" Amy said in her usual lighthearted mood.

"Amy, it's me." Kim's voice was weak and shaky.

"Kim, what's wrong?"

"Amy, I'm in real trouble. Can you come and see me?"

"What's wrong? You're scaring me."

"Please, I'm begging you, Amy. Come and help me."

"Okay, I'm coming, Kim. I'll be there tomorrow morning. Should I call Nathan for you?"

"No, no don't call him. I'll be okay. Just get here as soon as you can. Bye."

Amy was coming. It gave Kim hope and the strength she needed to get cleaned up. She crawled back to the bathroom, turned on the shower, and climbed in partially clothed. She curled up in a ball and laid there until the hot water was gone. *Tomorrow will be better. My friend will be here.*

Amy knocked on the door. There was no response, so she pounded harder. "Kim, are you in there?" Still no answer, but she thought she heard something. "Kim, it's Amy. Are you there?" she repeated louder this time.

Kim, trying hard to shake off the grogginess of a bad night's sleep, stumbled to the door. "Amy!" she said, throwing her arms around her friend's neck and holding on like a drowning person clinging to a life buoy. "I'm so glad you're here. Thank you, thank you for coming."

By late afternoon, neither of them had any more tears to cry, and Kim was spent—physically and emotionally—having shared every detail of the awful story.

"What am I going to do Amy?" she asked. "I can't tell Mom, it will break her heart; and my dad, well, you know how he is. If he finds out, I'll be disowned, and he'll never speak to me again. That would be the end of college."

"Are you absolutely sure there is no future with Nathan?"

"Two days ago, I would have told you that he was my one true love. I thought he was going to ask me to marry him. I loved him with all my heart, and I was sure that he loved me. Today, I feel totally empty. It's like I have this huge tear in my heart that can't be fixed and I'm bleeding to death. And after what I saw in his eyes last night, I never want to see him again. I have never felt such hate from any person or been so scared before."

"I don't know what to do either, Kim, but I do know that it's a decision you'll have to make for yourself. You're the one who's going to have to live with it for the rest of your life."

"How long can you stay, Amy? I just don't feel like I can be alone right now."

"I don't have to be back for work until Monday morning, so I'll stay until late Sunday afternoon. That will give us three days. Maybe by then we'll have this figured out."

Amy headed back that Sunday afternoon with nothing resolved. Kim was, in the end, completely alone; not even a kindred spirit could make this decision any easier. She felt she was left with only two terrible choices: drop out of college and have this baby on her own, or get an abortion. She had no way of supporting herself, much less caring for a new baby. Child support—if she could get it—and welfare, using her calculator, added up to a one-bedroom trailer on the wrong side of the tracks. She knew her father would never agree to help, and her dream of college would probably be gone forever. In the church that Kim attended with her mother, she had heard the preacher say that every life was sacred, including the unborn. How could a man possibly understand how a woman in my position feels? she reasoned. The scales of decision were slowly tilting down on the side of termination.

***

Kim's appointment at the clinic was set for 8:00 a.m. The procedure would take place at approximately 9:00 a.m., shortly after she was prepped. Then, like magic, the problem would disappear, and she would feel a tremendous sense of relief as her life returned to normal. At least that's the way the clinic counselor made it sound.

She pulled into the parking lot a little before 8:00, turned off the motor and reached for the door handle, then froze. "Come on, Kim," she said to herself. "Open the door and get this over with." But her body was not responding to her command. She leaned forward, resting her head against the steering wheel. Two unrelenting forces battled for her heart and mind, and she was caught in the middle, being ripped apart. Sobbing uncontrollably, she screamed, "What's wrong with me? I have to do this." Her outburst silenced the voices long enough for her to once again gain control. She sat up, took a deep breath, and wiped the tears away. She then forced herself out of the car and through the clinic doors where a cold, antiseptic-smelling room eerily greeted her. Except for Amy, she would tell no one of this sad day or the dark secret it held.

The days, weeks, and months rolled by, but Kim seldom ventured far from her apartment. She attended classes, bought groceries and gas once a week, attended an occasional study group, and on a rare occasion made a trip to the mall with a girlfriend. She never set foot in Starbucks again; her small coffeemaker in the apartment would have to do. Study, once again, became a refuge that offered relief from the thoughts plaguing her mind in the quiet. And Amy's nightly calls provided a lifeline, keeping Kim's head above water.

Kim dropped her American Lit class, and if she caught a glimpse of Nathan coming her way, she would immediately turn and walk in another direction. She had no desire to hear what he might say, or ever again look into those eyes. Once she saw him walking across campus with his right arm wrapped tightly around some girl's waist and her left hand neatly tucked away in the back pocket of his designer jeans. *Oh how I wish I could warn her*, she thought. That was the last time she saw him. As far as she knew, he didn't return for his junior year.

The cherry blossom trees were in full bloom signaling the end of a long cold winter Kim couldn't wait to forget. She would turn twenty in July, but the reflection she saw in the mirror looked much older to her. Thank God, summer vacation had arrived—and none too soon.

To Kim's surprise, she found herself longing for the simple life of Elk Grove. When she arrived, the route to her house took her past Poppa's Pizza and Billy's Bowling World. She laughed at herself as she passed by. Those places that she once detested now seemed more like old friends, rich with stories and warm memories.

How things had changed in the nine months she had been gone; even her dad seemed different as he welcomed her with open arms. Perhaps her absence had made his heart grow fonder. And her mother, well, their conversation began with a hug at the front door and ended with another hug just before 1:00 a.m. when they were both too tired to keep their eyes open a moment longer.

Kim didn't miss a Sunday morning church service with her mother that whole summer. When she was younger, church was a place to meet with friends and talk about boys, but it was much more than that now. What once seemed dull and uninteresting had become a source of strength. Perhaps she was beginning to understand why her mother felt so strongly about being involved.

The last thing on Kim's mind that summer was boys, but late in the summer, a young man walked up to her in the parking lot after a church service with a big smile on his face.

"Kim, do you remember me?" he asked.

"Mike...Mike Anderson? Is that you?" The lanky, insecure, late bloomer she had blown off in high school no longer fit that description.

"Yep, it's me. Nice to see you again."

"Nice to see you, too, Mike," she said, opening the door to the car where her mother was waiting. She was surprised to realize that she meant it.

"Amy told me you were in town and were heading back to college soon."

"Yeah, I leave next week."

"Well then, hope you have a nice trip and great year."

"Thanks Mike, I will."

Kim's annual dental appointment was scheduled for Friday morning at 9:00, the day before she would leave to begin her sophomore year. "Your teeth look great," the dentist said after viewing the X-rays and doing a quick exam. "Unless you have any questions or concerns, I'll turn you over to my dental assistant and she'll do the cleaning." He called for the assistant and then moved on to the patient in the next room.

As Kim lay in the chair waiting, she could clearly hear every word that was spoken between the dentist and her neighbor-patient. The flimsy dividers did little to muffle the sound throughout the office. From the gurgling of a suction tube and the sound of drilling, it was obvious that the other patient was having her tooth filled. Within seconds, Kim's body began shivering, like a person nearing hypothermia. As her heart raced and breathing quickened, she realized she was hyperventilating.

"I can't stay here; I've got to go," she said to the assistant.

"What's wrong?"

"Nothing, nothing. I'm sorry, but I have to get out of here—now."

Kim leapt from the dental chair, ripped off the bib, grabbed her purse, and raced from the building. Once inside her car and all alone, she broke down and cried, wailed really. The high pitched whine coming from the drill and the hollow suction of the vacuum tube combined with the antiseptic smell had, in her mind, propelled her back in time to the memory of a surgical suite that she had tried desperately to forget. "My god, how will I ever be able to sit in a dentist chair again?"

Within a few minutes, she regained control and went back into the dentist office just long enough to pay the bill. She had created quite a stir on the way out so she mentally prepared an answer for the inevitable questions. When the dental assistant asked if she was okay, Kim answered, "Yeah, I'm fine. I just had a little panic attack, that's all. I've never liked the dentist chair." That was enough to satisfy everyone's curiosity, and it prevented the inevitable call to her parents that would have most certainly launched an inquisition by her father. This episode also remained a secret to everyone, except Amy.

Kim, Amy, and Kim's mother had become experts at packing the Honda. They crammed more into the trunk and backseat than even they thought possible. The trunk lid closed easily enough, but Kim had to sit in the front seat and pull everything toward her away from the passenger door so Amy could close it from the outside. Job done. Hot chocolate with lots of marshmallows would keep them satisfied till the wee hours of the morning when their conversation was finally overpowered by the need for sleep. Reluctantly, they said goodnight, and Kim went straight to bed where she quickly fell into a deep sleep.

At 4:30 a.m. Kim bolted up right in bed, with eyes wide open, heart racing, and sweating as if a fever of 103 had just broken. "Oh God, it's only a dream," she gasped.

She had seen herself standing in a field, waist deep in the most beautiful array of orchids, lilies and roses imaginable. The rich, yet delicate fragrance of a floral shop filled the air. Near the crest of a distant hill she could just make out someone sitting in a chair, beckoning her to come. As she walked through the tall grass and flowers, the sun's warmth draped over her shoulders, while the cool breeze gently blew her long hair across her face.

Closer now, she could see that the chair was a rocking chair, and the person in it was a young woman lovingly looking down at a nursing child she held close. She motioned with her hand for Kim to come closer yet, until she was standing just in front of them. Kim reached out and gently stroked the baby's cheek with one finger. The baby responded by grasping Kim's little finger with her tiny hand. *This must be heaven,* she thought.

The child's mother slowly raised her head. Kim shrieked and jumped back. Kim felt as though she was looking into a mirror—but it was no reflection. Drifts of deep snow instantly covered the field, while billowing gray clouds filled the sky and a bitter wind sliced through her thin gown. The young mother, Kim, sat wrapped in a tattered blanket in a broken rocker. Tears from hollow eyes coursed down deep creases in her cheeks.

In an instant, the dream was over and Kim was wide awake. Shaking, she reached for the lamp next to her bed, nearly knocking it over as she struggled to turn on the light that would drive the darkness, and hopefully, the fear, from the room. Then she lay back on her pillow knowing there would be no more sleep that night. Her mind replayed the dream over and over again. The tears that now trickled from the corner of her eyes down the sides of her face and onto the pillow were no longer tears of fear. They were tears borne of heartache that comes only from the loss of a beloved child.

The chime of the grandfather clock in the living room woke Kim from a semi-conscious state. It was completely dark in the room now and the six chimes reminded her that Mike would be home within the hour. She reached for the switch on the lamp next to the sofa and then hesitated, drawing her arm back under the blanket. Something was different; she felt as though there was a tangible presence of God in the room. Waves of His love began sweeping over her soul.

She had experienced a similar feeling as a child when her mother would hold her in her lap, gently stroke her hair, and tell her how much she was loved. But this went much deeper. It was an impression; but more than that—a powerful sense of an unconditional love that went far beyond any natural human experience. She sat quietly, not wanting to break the spell. She allowed her mind to drift back in time.

The recurring nightmare had become less frequent over time as Kim numbed to its effect. But it always remained just under the surface of her consciousness, waiting for the right stimulus to arouse it. She had learned to avoid the kinds of experiences that would bring it to the surface: holding a newborn, attending baby showers, even going to parks and playgrounds. When asked about children, she simply replied, "I don't really think I'm the maternal type."

The next three years passed quickly. Kim graduated with a bachelor of arts degree in English and a minor in American history. She completed her student teaching in the last term of her senior year at a junior high school near the college. When the Elk Grove school district received her application for a teaching position, they wasted no time in replying. It was difficult to recruit good teachers to a small town, so when one of their own expressed interest, the district went all out to secure her services.

Kim accepted the district's terms without hesitation. The fast-paced chaotic life of the big city, which Kim could not wait to experience only four short years earlier, no longer held any appeal. She packed up and moved back home where she planned to stay.

Amy was planning to get married that summer, and Kim was to be the maid of honor. Amy's fiancé, Scott, had asked Mike Anderson, his closest friend since high school, to be his best man. It was Scott who had goaded Mike into asking Kim for that date in their senior year—just to keep Mike from talking about Kim all the time. He thought that would be the best way to put Mike out of his misery, and it worked. Mike never mentioned her name again.

Mike graduated from a local junior college with an associate's degree in business, which marked the end of his formal education. The on-the-job training that he received from his father was far more valuable than any classroom studies. He grew up learning his father's farm implement business, and now that Dad was fighting for his life against liver cancer, it was up to him and his mother to run the business.

"Hi Valerie, I'll have my usual," Mike said to the waitress as he plopped down on a stool at the counter of Martha's Cafe. Almost like a ritual, the locals gathered there for breakfast to hash over the intrusion of big government into their business, the weather, and the price of corn and cattle.

"How's your dad doing, Mike?" asked the pastor, who was often there for breakfast himself. He was a close personal friend of Mike's father, and a day seldom passed without a visit to his bedside.

"Not real good," Mike answered sadly, "but he sure appreciates your visits, and so do my mom and I. Thank you."

Mike left the cafe to head to his next destination. He only had to travel a few miles and then walk about one hundred yards through a small cornfield to his personal duck blind hidden among the bushes next to the river. Most of the outsiders who hunted using these duck blinds were paying the local farmers big bucks for the privilege. Hunting was a passion of Mike's for sure, but the duck blind also served as his place of solitude. Many of the important decisions of his life had been made among the snow-covered corn stocks of that blind that he and his dad had so often occupied together. He dreamed of bringing his own son to this special place one day.

During Amy and Scott's rehearsal dinner, Kim found herself sitting next to Mike. No doubt, this had been orchestrated by Scott and Amy since they had painstakingly arranged the place cards. Kim smiled at Amy as Mike helped Kim find her seat. Perhaps he had been in on the plan as well, she thought.

Mike seemed a little uncomfortable in a sport coat and tie. His usual attire was Wrangler jeans with a big belt, cowboy boots and a black polo shirt with "Anderson Farm Implements" embroidered in gold on the left side neatly tucked in his trousers. He would wear a sport coat to church from time to time but that was about the extent of it. He was a man who was very comfortable in his own skin and never felt a need to impress anyone. Well, almost never; sitting next to Kim may have been the exception.

Their conversation focused on the bride and groom initially and then gradually shifted to questions about each other's life since high school. They were enjoying themselves so much that they had to be reminded when it was time to make their speeches and offer a toast.

When the formalities were over, dinner devoured, and they were down to the last few bites of sherbet ice cream, Mike thought he would give it another try.

"Kim, I was wondering if you might consider having dinner with me sometime."

Kim looked at him for a moment and then smiled. "You know what, Mike? I think I would really like that."

"How about Saturday evening after the wedding?" Mike said hopefully.

"Sure, that'll work."

Driving home that night, Kim was a little surprised at how quickly she had agreed to this date. Since Nathan, there had been no one, and she would never forget how easily she had been deceived by him. This country boy, however, was very transparent and had a genuine kindness that was obviously rooted deep in the heart. And in Elk Grove, as everyone knew, there were no secrets. If he had a questionable reputation, she would have heard about it by now. Besides, Amy thought he was a great guy. And she knew she could trust Amy.

When she agreed to dinner Kim had no idea that Mike planned to do the cooking. She had to give him credit; it was a novel approach to a first date.

The main course on the dinner menu was roast duck, one he had brought down with a 20 gauge that very morning. Mike's mother had prepared duck for dinner a hundred times. How hard could it be?

When Kim arrived the table was neatly set with fine china, wine glasses, and silverware borrowed from Mike's mom. Mike pulled the dinner chair out and slid it back under her as she sat down. "Would you like a glass of wine before dinner?"

"That sounds great," Kim said.

"Have you ever eaten roasted wild duck before?"

"No, I haven't, is that what we are having tonight?"

"Yes, it's great, you'll love it."

Mike smiled and walked confidently across the kitchen. He opened the oven door and the excitement began. A cloud of smoke boiled out and up to the ceiling. "Uh-oh," he said. The words were hardly out of his mouth before the smoke alarm started squealing. Mike pulled the smoking duck out of the oven and threw it into the sink. He grabbed a towel and began frantically fanning the smoke detector. As he did so he backed into the table, lost his balance, and reached for one corner to brace himself. The table tipped toward him, and he went flying to the floor. Everything that had been placed so carefully, including two glasses of wine and the candle, ended up in his lap.

Kim jumped back. "Are you okay?"

Mike rolled his eyes and smiled. "How would you feel about a delivery from Poppa's Pizza?" They both burst into laughter.

———————————◦◦◦◦————————————

Monday morning, Kim reported for her first day of work at Elk Grove Elementary. She originally applied for a teaching position at the junior high level, but the school district needed help at the second and third grade level, so she accepted that position with the hope of moving up the following year. In two short weeks, the classrooms would be abuzz with rambunctious boys and chatty girls. Before classes began in earnest, Kim was completely occupied attending staff meetings, reviewing and preparing curriculum, learning the expectations of the administrators and other teachers who would act as mentors, and then meeting parents at evening orientations.

Ready or not, the first day of school arrived, and the second-grade students poured into her classroom—all thirty two of them. Kim felt a bit overwhelmed at first, but by the end of the day she had assigned desks, passed out books, and learned a little about each student. She was erasing the chalkboard after class when Mrs. Robinson, the vice principal, walked in.

"How was your first day, Kim?"

"I think it went pretty well," she said confidently.

"Great, glad to hear it. We need an additional teacher to monitor the playground for afternoon recess, so would you take care of that please?"

"Sure, I would be glad to," Kim said with an eagerness to please. "Is there anything else?"

"No, that's all for now. Thank you, see ya tomorrow."

Perhaps Amy was right. Perhaps time was her friend, and she was beginning to heal. The haunting nightmare had remained asleep for over a year, and the fear that being around children might awaken it had nearly faded.

To Kim's relief, the weeks and months passed without any signs of the demon showing its ugly head, and she was becoming more comfortable with the children every day. "I guess I was created to be a teacher," she would often tell Mike. "I love teaching; I can see myself doing this for the rest of my life."

Her relationship with Mike was moving forward as well. They were seeing each other every weekend and often attended church together. Mike would confide his thoughts about Kim to Scott, who then informed Amy, who then passed every detail along to Kim. Always the truth, never a secret. What Kim was learning about Mike through the grapevine (which in Elk Grove was faster than high-speed internet) continued to validate the sincerity of his behavior and words. Being a gentleman was not at all role-play for Mike; he truly was a gentleman. He treated Kim like a princess—not to impress her, but because to him, she was one. There was passion and there was chemistry, but never once did he ask her to compromise. Had he, Kim would have ended the relationship, and Mike knew it. She had decided that there would never again be a wedding night without first a wedding day.

Kim had dreamed of a June wedding many times, but the reality proved to be even better than the dream. On a sunny afternoon, two years to the day after that unforgettable first date, Kim walked gracefully down the aisle, arm in arm with her father. She would remember everything—the fragrance of the bouquet she held, the simple beauty of the rose petals the flower girl had carefully dropped in the aisle, the warm smile of each family member and friend as she walked by, and most importantly, the loving eyes of the one she adored waiting patiently for her at the altar. This kind and gentle man, the man who couldn't cook a duck, had somehow managed to win her heart and her hand in marriage.

Kim was so glad they hadn't waited any longer to be married. Mike's father, who dressed in several layers of clothing to help obscure the skeleton of his cancer-ridden body, had mustered enough strength to attend their wedding. Every time Kim visited him, he never failed to remind her how thankful he was that Mike had found such a wonderful woman. At the reception, just before the bride and groom headed to the waiting limo, he asked to speak to Kim privately.

"Kim, I just wanted to tell you that I've never seen Mike so happy. I know that God brought you to him, and I am so thankful and happy for the two of you." Tears begin to fill his eyes as he took Kim's hand. "Sure wish I could be here to see my grandchildren."

He went home to heaven two months later.

Mike loved children; so much so that from time to time, he would drop by the school during recess and help Kim in the playground. "When we have a little boy," he would say, "I'll take him hunting with me in the evenings after school." Or, "If we have a girl, let's put her hair in pigtails like that little girl on the teeter-totter." They talked about children often enough, but Kim always kept the conversation in future tense, even though they would soon be celebrating their fourth anniversary.

One night, as they lay in bed, Mike asked Kim a direct question: "Is there some reason you don't want to have children?"

Kim knew that question was coming sooner or later, so she had rehearsed her answer many times. "It's not that I don't want children. I want to have a family with you, but I'm just not ready yet. Can you please just accept that for now?"

Mike didn't respond in words. He simply wrapped his arms around Kim and gave her a soft kiss on the cheek. In his heart, he knew there must be some deep sorrow in her life that was related to children and that either she could not or was just unwilling to share it with him. Although it hurt to be excluded from this part of her life, he would never insist upon knowing. Kim was relieved the conversation had gone no further.

That night she had a dream; it was much different than the recurring dream she had before, but just as haunting. She saw herself sitting at a kitchen table surrounded by laughing children. In the middle of the table was a round double- layered cake. The first layer was decorated with pink roses, and the second, multi-colored balloons. On top were five pink candles strategically placed under the five letters of a little girl's name. It read, "Happy Birthday Grace."

It was time to make a wish and blow out the candles. Grace closed her eyes, said something quietly and then took a big breath and blew out all the candles in one try. Everybody cheered. The noise soon subsided as the children devoured the cake and ice cream. Kim walked around to the other side of the table and sat next to Grace. She bent down and whispered, "Can you tell me what you wished?"

Grace looked up at her quizzically as though she knew something that Kim did not. Then she grinned and got up on her knees so she could whisper quietly. She pushed Kim's hair aside and pressed her lips next to her ear. "I wished this wasn't a dream, Mommy." In the next moment, the children were gone and Kim was wide awake.

Although Mike lay only inches away, she felt completely alone. This dream did not re-awaken old fears but rather created a sorrow and heartache rooted deep in an overpowering sense of loss. She put her hand over her mouth to hold back the sound of a cry that emanated from within her soul. There was no doubt in her mind; she had just looked into the eyes of the daughter she had never known.

For the next two weeks the dream woke her every night and left her unable to fall back to sleep. She began staying up late grading papers and working on curriculum, hoping that sheer exhaustion would bring a deep sleep that the dream could not penetrate. Even that was unsuccessful, yet she could not bring herself to tell Mike. Shame and self-loathing was keeping the padlock on the door of her secret secured.

The dark shadows forming under Kim's bloodshot eyes could no longer be concealed with makeup. She often stared at her food, moving it from place to place on the plate, scarcely taking a bite. Her conversations with Mike had been replaced with long spans of silence, a sure sign that something was seriously wrong. Sleep deprivation was taking its toll, and Mike was worried. He held her next to him on the sofa in the evenings hoping she would fall asleep, but it didn't help. When he tried to persuade her to talk about it, she'd answer, "It's just one of those female things; I'll be fine." Eventually, she'd go to bed where she would quietly cry herself to sleep, only to be awakened once again by the unrelenting dream.

One Saturday night, the dream of Grace blowing out the candles was replaced with the other more terrifying dream of the young mother sitting in the rocking chair on the side of the hill. Kim had thought it was gone forever, and now it had come back with a vengeance that felt like an all-out assault intended to drive her insane. She crawled out of bed and made her way to the den where she closed the door and, out of desperation, called Amy.

"Amy, it's me."

"What's wrong?" Amy replied.

"I can't take it anymore. That awful nightmare is back, and I feel like I'm going crazy. What should I do?"

"Have you told Mike?"

"No, you know I can't tell him."

"Kim, listen to me. You cannot go on like this. Tomorrow, I'm going to take you to see your mother, and you're going to tell her everything. I know you think the truth will break her heart, but she's stronger than that, and I have a feeling she'll help you."

"Okay, if you think I should, I'll do it. It can't be any worse than what I'm feeling now. I'll see you at church tomorrow."

Kim went back to bed and was able to manage a few hours of sleep. In the morning, she and Mike went to church as usual and then to lunch with Scott and Amy. At lunch, Amy put the plan into motion.

"Hey Mike," she said, "why don't you come over and watch the game at our house with Scott this afternoon? Kim and I want to do a little shopping and then go by and visit with her mother for a while."

"Sounds good to me. Are you sure you feel up to that, Kim?"

"Sure, I'll be fine."

After the men were settled, Amy drove Kim straight to her parents' house.

"This seemed like a good idea last night, Amy, but now that I'm actually here, I'm really scared. Would you come with me?"

"Not this time. This is something you need to do by yourself."

"I guess you're right. Well, at least pray for me."

"I will."

Kim walked to the front door as Amy drove away. She didn't know if it was from exhaustion or fear, but her hand was shaking almost uncontrollably as she reached to ring the doorbell. Without waiting for someone to answer she walked in as she had done thousands of times before.

"Is that you Kim?" she heard her mother ask.

"Yes, it's me," she said softly, trying to control her emotions.

Kim walked to the kitchen where her mother was finishing washing the dishes. Her father had already retired to the living room where he was watching the football game.

"Mom, I need to talk to you."

Kim's mother turned around, and the smile on her face immediately turned to one of serious concern. She set the towel down and walked over to Kim, putting her arms around her. "What is it, honey?" she asked.

Kim's whole body was shaking. "Take my hand," her mother said. "Let's go to the bedroom where you can lie down and tell me what's going on."

"Thanks, Mom."

Kim's mother helped her onto the bed and covered her with a light blanket. Then she sat down next to her and gently wiped away Kim's tears with her hand.

"Now tell me, what's wrong?"

"I'll tell you Mom, but please don't interrupt until I've finished, no matter what. Okay?"

"Yes, of course."

Kim sat up, leaned back against the headboard, and took a deep breath. "Here goes." She then launched into the story, beginning with meeting Nathan. She told how she had fallen in love with him and that she was sure he loved her too. Then, she dropped the bomb. "Mom, I got pregnant." She waited for a moment, expecting to hear a response from her mother. Kim's mom closed her eyes and then nodded as if to say, Go on, I'm listening. "I was so sure that Nathan was going to marry me and everything would be okay. But in the end, I realized that he was only using me. I wanted to tell you, Mom, I did. But I couldn't. I knew it would break your heart just like it's doing right now, and I knew that Dad would be so ashamed of me that he would disown me.

"I can't describe how alone and scared I felt that night after Nathan totally rejected me and our baby. I couldn't sleep. I couldn't eat. I literally felt like I could go crazy. If it hadn't been for Amy, I don't know what I would have done. I felt like there was no way out, and so finally I decided to get an abortion. I'm so ashamed to say this now, but when it was over, I actually felt relieved at first. I didn't know it would come back to haunt me.

"It's been almost ten years now and I really thought I was over it, but the last few weeks have become unbearable. I feel like I'm going crazy."

Tears were now streaming down her mother's cheeks as Kim continued. Anger that Kim had never expressed erupted like a volcano as she lashed out at her father and blamed him for making it impossible to tell the truth. "Why does Daddy have to be so black and white about everything? He expects me to be perfect, and no matter how hard I try I know that nothing I do will ever please him."

After three light taps on the bedroom door, it slowly opened, revealing the looming presence of her father. It stopped her cold. He walked in and sat on the loveseat facing the bed. "I saw that you were upset when you came in so I followed the two of you to the bedroom and have been listening just outside the door."

"It's okay, honey," her mother said. "Keep going; we both need to hear what you have to say."

Kim continued with the stories of the dreams, the sleepless nights, and how all of this was beginning to affect her relationship with Mike. Years of torment and pain that had been held back like a dam were being released in a flood of emotions, words, and tears. And when she finished her story, she put her head in her hands and sobbed. "How could God ever forgive someone who would take the life of their own child?"

Kim's mom wrapped her arms around her daughter's shoulders and began to stroke her head as she had so many times when she was a child. Kim wept. "I'm so sorry, I'm so sorry."

Kim's mother held her while she cried. When Kim's crying finally subsided, her mother took a deep breath. "Kim, I'm sorry that we weren't there for you and that our attitudes made it impossible for you to tell us what you were facing. If there is anyone who needs to be forgiven, it's us. "

Kim's father hadn't moved a muscle. He was leaning forward, sitting with his elbows on his thighs and his face buried in his hands as he stared at the floor. The gavel of judgment and condemnation that Kim was expecting had still not fallen.

"I have something I want to show you," Kim's mother said. She walked to the dresser, opened the second drawer, and reached under the clothes for a small, flat box. Holding the box, she walked back to Kim's side and sat down. "Open this," she said, handing the box to Kim.

Kim opened the box to find a gold heart attached to a necklace. "Read what it says," her mother said.

Kim read it aloud, "I love you, Heather." Then she turned it over and read, "'I love you, Mommy.' It's beautiful, but who is Heather?"

"Your father and I have a secret too, one that we've kept hidden far too long. When you were three years old, I became pregnant again. We were facing difficult times, both financially and in our marriage, so...."

"Ann..." her father interrupted. "Let me tell her, I owe her that. It was me, Kim," he said. "It's my fault. Your mom is just trying to protect me by talking about our financial difficulties and marriage problems. Yes, we were having problems, but that was no excuse for what I did. I persuaded your mother to get an abortion."

Kim was stunned; she could hardly believe what she was hearing.

He slowly stood up, then walked over and knelt down in front of them. Holding Kim's hands tightly in his, he began to cry.

"Heather is the name your mother gave to our daughter," he explained, barely getting the words out. "Your mom has dreamed of your sister many times." He looked at his wife. "Ann, I have never told you this, but I have dreamed of her many times too. I've regretted what I did every day since the abortion, and now I can see that it has come back to break all of our hearts. I'm sorry, I am so sorry," he repeated as he wept.

Kim's mother dropped to her knees on the floor next to her husband's side and wrapped her arms around him.

"Daddy," Kim said softly. She had never seen him cry.

Kim's father continued, "Kim, you served as a constant reminder of the child I had so easily let go. I hated myself for my awful decision to pressure you mother. While I was sitting here listening to you, I realized how different our relationship would have been had I not tried to force you to live the life that I could never live myself. If I had shown you the love and affection you needed, perhaps you would never have looked to that young man. At the very least, you wouldn't have been left all alone to make a decision that no woman should ever be asked to make. You would have a child, and we would have a grandchild." He began weeping aloud once again, struggling to speak. "My self-ishness has cost the lives of two children."

He raised his head and looked Kim in the eyes. "I'm sorry for what I've done to you, Kim. Please, can you ever forgive me?" Kim slid to the floor next to him, and they cried together, as years of resentment and anger evaporated like fog on a sunny morning.

"Daddy," Kim said as she threw her arms around him, "I love you."

Her father looked her in the eyes. "Kim, I've never told you how I feel about you. But you are the most wonderful daughter a father could ever ask for. I'm so proud of you and all that you have accomplished in your life. I should have told you that so many years ago. I love you too, very much." He then stood up, kissed her on the forehead and left the room as quietly as he had come in.

Kim turned to her mother, now sitting on the bed, and asked her, "Mom, please, please tell me, how have you been able to live with this secret all these years?"

"It was terrible at first," her mother answered. "I had the same feelings that you are experiencing until I realized God had forgiven me." She smiled.

"Mom," Kim said, "how can you know that?"

"After the abortion," she began, "when what I had done really sank in, I was so depressed I actually thought about suicide, and it scared me. I was so desperate, I launched into a search for the truth. I was hoping to find an answer that would relieve the guilt and pain. That's when I began looking for God. I started reading the Bible and visiting churches.

"I had heard about Jesus all my life and thought that He was all about rules and judgment and punishment. But Kim, God is not like a father who you can never please. He loves us just the way we are, and He loves us in spite of our worst mistakes. The more I got to know Him, the more I realized how much He loves me. And His love is what made it possible for me to forgive myself. That was the hardest part of all.

"I also realized that God had forgiven your father and I needed to do the same. It wasn't entirely his fault; I could have refused the abortion. Forgiving him brought an even greater understanding of God's forgiveness toward me.

"I don't completely understand it yet, but what I do know is that God forgave me for everything I have ever done—not just the abortion, but everything. When I realized that, I found peace." Her face almost glowed as she talked about her love for God.

"Mom, I want to believe what you're saying," she interrupted, "but I feel so terrible; I feel like a murderer."

"I understand, honey, I felt like that too. But forgiveness is not about a feeling. Forgiveness is real Kim. Whether you feel like it or not or think you deserve it or not, He has already forgive you of the abortion."

"God has a way of turning our worst mistakes into miracles. I read in the Bible that He knew us before we were in our mother's womb. That means He also knew our children before they were in ours. We can be sure that He knows them now and that they are with Him in heaven. Life doesn't end with a physical death, no matter how or when that happens; it continues eternally. I don't think about what Heather's life would have been like here on earth anymore. Instead, I imagine what it must be like for her in heaven now. And one day I will be joining her there."

Hope replaced despair, and Kim's eyes lit up. "I know that's right, Mom. I know it in my heart. You really believe Heather is in heaven, don't you?"

"Yes, absolutely! Not only do I believe she's in heaven, but I believe she's anxiously awaiting our arrival. In my dreams I have seen her many times, and she's not angry, she's happy. I'm not sure how this works, but I ask God to tell her that I love her, and I'm convinced she gets the messages."

"Mom, I think I have a daughter too, and I want to name her Grace. That's the name that was on the birthday cake in my dream."

"Then from now on, we'll call her Grace."

***

It was after 10:00 p.m. when Kim finally called Amy. Mike was still waiting at their house for her call. Amy had let him know that Kim was talking to her mother about the problems she was having sleeping. He could only hope that it would help.

"Amy, would you ask Mike to come get me?"

"Sure. Is everything okay?"

"You were right Amy, my mom did help. What's happened is absolutely wonderful. But I'm too exhausted to talk about it tonight; can I tell you about it tomorrow?"

"I can hardly wait to hear. We'll talk tomorrow. Mike's already on his way."

"Kim, you seem different. What happened this afternoon?" Mike asked as they drove home.

"What has happened to me is amazing, and it's also more than I can process. I'm not sure I can even express it right now. I need a little time to think it all through. Would it be okay if I wait till you come home from work tomorrow to tell you the whole story?"

"As much as I want to know right now, I can certainly wait one more day. I love ya, babe."

The beams from Mike's headlights startled Kim as he pulled into the driveway. The sound of the garage door opening somehow served as a signal for her heart to start racing. Within a few seconds, it was beating so hard and fast that she could feel the veins in her neck pulsing. Kim thought she was prepared, but now that the moment of truth had come, her mind was filled with doubts and questions. "Be strong Kim," she reassured herself. "You can do this."

Mike often told Kim, "I know I don't deserve you, but I love you with all my heart and I always will." Tonight she would be counting on the truth of those words. Mike was completely head over heels in love with her and more than willing to overlook what Kim jokingly referred to as her slight imperfections. In spite of those faults, he had placed her on a pedestal of virtue, and she about to step down.

The garage door was closing, and in some strange way it was as if time had slowed to a crawl. Dozens of crystal clear thoughts raced through Kim's mind as she threw the blanket aside and made those few short steps to the back door. Their fourth anniversary would be this Friday, and she knew Mike had already made secret plans. *I hope what I'm about to say doesn't ruin those plans.*

She smiled and gave Mike a big kiss. "I'm ready to talk," she said. Kim took him by the hand and led him to the sofa where she had been sitting for the last several hours. If fear and excitement can exist at the same time in the same body, that is exactly what Kim was feeling.

Mike took off his boots and laid his jacket across the arm of the chair. "Just wanted to get comfortable; I've got a feeling this might take awhile."

"You're right, it probably will. I think I should start by telling you about the dream I had last night."

"It was a good one, I hope."

Kim smiled. "Yes, it really was," she said excitedly. "As it began, I saw myself entering heaven. I was young, younger than I am now. It was an indescribable place arrayed with flowers and trees that I have never seen before and fragrances that I have never smelled on this earth. Light seemed to be coming from everywhere but not from anywhere specific. I was walking on what looked like a path of gold that felt soft under my feet like a plush carpet. There were animals of all kinds everywhere, and lions and lambs were lying down together, just like the Bible says. The peace I felt was like nothing I've ever known."

"I looked up, and in the distance I could see someone running toward me. As we came closer together, I could see that it was a little girl about five years old with long blonde hair. She was dressed in a pearl white gown that shimmered in the light, and she had the warmest, most inviting smile you could ever imagine. She ran toward me faster and faster, and when she got close enough I bent down just in time for her to jump into my arms."

"At that moment, she said, 'Mommy, I've been waiting for you.' We began to laugh and cry at the same time as we twirled around and around. When we stopped, I put her down and she took me by the hand. 'Come with me Mommy,' she said, 'I have something to show you.' Then, as we began to walk, the dream ended."

"Mike, that little girl was my daughter. It was like a heavenly reunion, a joyful reunion with the daughter I had never known on earth." Kim's eyes became moist with tears of joy.

"Wow! What do you think it means, honey?" Mike asked.

"I know exactly what it means. I have a daughter, Mike, and she is in heaven."

Mike's imagination was operating at breakneck speed, taking him for a ride through a minefield of possibilities. "I'm not sure I'm following you. What daughter are you talking about?" he asked.

Kim reached over and put her hand on his shoulder. "I can image what you must be thinking right now, but just let me finish and it will all make sense to you."

"Okay, you've got my attention. Go ahead."

"I know you've been worried and wondered what's been making me so crazy these last few weeks. And it's time that I tell you. There's a secret from my past that I've kept locked away for nearly ten years. I had planned to keep it a secret for the rest of my life, until yesterday. The change that you said you saw in me last night is real, and it's what has given me the freedom and the courage to tell you what happened.

"Mike you're the one I love; the one person I should have been able to trust with this secret, and still, I kept it from you. I'm so sorry for that, and I can only hope that after you hear it, you will be able to forgive me."

Kim took her time, telling the entire story from the day she left for college up to the last few hours that she had spent sitting on the sofa staring out the window. When she was finished, she moved closer to Mike and took his hand. "Can you ever forgive me?" she asked.

"This explains so much," Mike began. "And listening to you talk about it is setting me free, too."

Kim interrupted, "What do you mean?"

"I've been tormented with the thought that you really didn't love me and that was why you couldn't or wouldn't talk to me," he answered.

Kim leaned close to him and passionately kissed his lips. "My darling, Mike," she said. "I'm sorry, that's so not true. I love you with all my heart."

"Kim, when I married you, I suspected that you might have some things in your past you didn't want to share. But you know what? It didn't matter to me when I married you. I loved you for who you were, and I still do.

"Now I understand all the sleeplessness and the many times I've heard you crying in the middle of the night. I always knew it was more than just some female thing, but I had no idea how deep the sorrow must have been that you were suffering. There were so many times that I wanted to press you for answers, but I was afraid it would push you away, and that was something I couldn't bear."

They clung to each other tightly as Mike continued. "I really understand now. I understand why you've been so evasive when it comes to talking about having a family. I can't image how hard it must have been for you to listen to me talk about what life was going to be like with our children."

"Mike, I wasn't avoiding the subject because I didn't want to have children with you," Kim interjected. "It was because I felt I didn't deserve to have children after what I had done."

"Then I have one question for you," he paused and smiled.

"What?" Kim responded.

"How would you like to give Grace a little brother or sister?"

"Yes," Kim said through tears of joy. "With everything that is in me, yes."

Mike leaned back against the pillow on the sofa and gave that mischievous smile she had seen so many times before.

"What are you thinking?" Kim asked.

"I was just thinking that this is going to be the most romantic anniversary ever."

"Amy," Kim said as she held the phone with one hand and rubbed her swollen belly with the other, "accepting the forgiveness of God is one thing, but forgiving yourself and living without self-condemnation is a whole other matter. I know my mom is there, and I believe I will be too. But it's taking far more time to see things the way God sees them than I imagined it would."

"Although it may seem like it's happening slowly," Amy replied, "I'm telling you, you're not the same person you were seven months ago. Older and wiser for sure, but the old Kim, my best friend, is finally back. And eight weeks from now, I'm going to be a godmother, Mike's going to be a dad, and Grace is going to be the sister of a beautiful baby boy. I can hardly wait!"

A Word from the Author on Forgiveness

In the story you've just read, Kim's mother said, "Forgiveness is not about a feeling. Forgiveness is real. Whether you feel like it or not or think you're worthy or not, God has already forgiven you of the abortion."

Kim's mother was finally able to forgive herself when she realized that she had already been forgiven by God. She came to the understanding that God was not upset with her for what she had done, that He loved her unconditionally, and that He was taking good care of her child in heaven.

We are all imperfect people who live in a corrupt world where we are motivated by our own fears, selfish desires, and interests. And on top of that, we are constantly bombarded by messages that feed our fears and drive us to fulfill those desires in all the wrong ways. That is why the Bible says that it's impossible for any human being to keep God's law.

We have all read or heard God's laws, but the ones most talked about are: you shall not murder, commit adultery, steal, bear false witness, or covet what others have. Some jokingly call these and a few more the "Big Ten," but there are many more than ten, far too many for us to remember, much less keep. Yet the Bible says that if we break even one of His laws it is as if we broke them all (James 2:10). No one is excluded from this group; we are all in the same boat.

Did you know that Christianity is the only faith in which you will find a Savior? All other religions are based on your performance, and many Christians have allowed that idea to creep into their philosophy. That's why people often say, "I sure hope the good I've done outweighs the bad." Fortunately, God's forgiveness isn't based on our performance at all. It's based on the sacrifice that Jesus made.

God came to earth and was born as a baby—Jesus. Although Jesus was God, He was also completely human. He was the only person who had the power to live a life without sin. He walked in our shoes; He understands our humanity, and He knows how we feel. He was tempted in every way, just as we are tempted, and yet never failed (Hebrews 4:15).

It was the sinless life Jesus lived that qualified Him to become the sacrifice for our sin. He was guilty of nothing, yet He was crucified. When Jesus was on the cross, the Bible says that He actually became sin for us. God's entire wrath was released upon Jesus, and when it was exhausted, Jesus said with a loud voice, "It is finished." At that moment, the price for our sins was paid in full so that we could be in right standing with God (2 Corinthians 5:21). This was, is, and always will be the greatest exchange that has ever taken place in history. And if we will reach out and accept this gift, realizing that it has absolutely nothing to do with our goodness, but God's love, then we will be reconciled to Him forever.

Kim's mother understood that Jesus didn't come to the earth to condemn us but to save us because He loved us (John 3:16-17). He didn't come as a judge but as a servant. In the Bible there's a story of a woman who was caught in the act of adultery and dragged to the feet of Jesus. Instead of condemning her, Jesus said to her accusers, "Whoever is without sin cast the first stone." They all walked away, and after they were gone Jesus said to the woman, "Neither do I condemn you, go and sin no more" (John 8:7-11).

Jesus told the woman to stop what she was doing because He loved her. He knew that adultery would destroy her life. God hates sin, but not for the reason that many people believe. He hates sin because it hurts people, and God loves people. When we allow Him to guide our lives, He will empower us to live the life that will result in great blessing and success.

God dealt with sin on the cross once and forever. All the sin that we have committed or ever will commit has been forgiven by God through the sacrifice of Jesus. And that includes abortion. There is absolutely nothing that we have done or ever will do that can separate us from God's unconditional love (Romans 8: 34-39).

The Bible says that if you will simply say with your mouth, out loud, that Jesus is the Son of God and believe in your heart that God raised Him from the dead, you will be saved, and He will be with you forever. There are no other conditions to meet; Salvation is a free gift that we can't earn. When Kim's mother finally understood that, it brought a freedom and love into her heart that she had never known. It will do the same for you.

I have no doubt. Every child that has been aborted or miscarried is in the presence of God. They are all alive and happy. They aren't mad at their parents and neither is God. They are excitedly awaiting their opportunity for a Joyful Reunion.

About the Author

Jim and Shirley Ertel recently celebrated their 43th wedding anniversary. Their son and daughter are both married and between the two, they have given them six grandchildren. Jim has been in the ministry for twenty five years serving in many capacities. He is the director of partner relations at Andrew Wommack Ministries and teaches on family relations at Charis Bible College. Jim and Shirley are also the founders of Heart of the Family Ministries. Their desire is to see families build strong foundations and bring restoration and reconciliation to those that are broken.

Jim is the author of *Contending for the Heart*, the hidden key to your child's behavior. It's written as a collection of short stories about real families who found that correct behavior naturally followed when they contend for and won the heart of their child.

HEART OF THE FAMILY

Vision:

Help establish strong families rooted and grounded in God's Word and bring reconciliation and restoration to those that are struggling and broken.

Mission:

Use every available communication medium to teach the truth of the Bible concerning families. Expose the lies and misconceptions the enemy uses to build walls within the home and destroy relationships. By the power of the Holy Spirit, open the doors to recociliation that will heal marriages and turn the hearts of the children to their parents and the parents to their children. Help families rebuild strong foundations that will withstand the storms of life.

Contact Jim and Shirley Ertel at:

Heart of the Family
P.O. Box 2063
Monument, CO 80132
Website: www.heartofthefamily.org
Email: info@heartofthefamily.org

Contending
for the
Heart

Parents are asking, "How can I control my children's behavior when they are being subjected to so many outside influences?" As reasonable as that question may seem, it's the wrong question. We should be asking, "How can I influence and win the heart of my child?" *Contending for the Heart* is a collection of short stories about real families who found that correct behavior naturally follows when you content for and win the heart of your child.

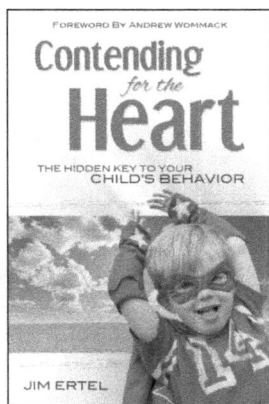

www.ingramcontent.com/pod-product-compliance
Lightning Source LLC
Chambersburg PA
CBHW071630040426
42452CB00009B/1562